Practice Guidebook for C Programming Language

S.ANBAZHAGAN

ISBN: 1540521915
ISBN-13: 978-1540521910

DEDICATION

This book is dedicated to the lotus feet of
THE MOTHER
&
SRI AUROBINDO.

CONTENTS

ACKNOWLEDGMENTS

First and foremost, I sincerely record my gratitude to god almighty for having bestowed this opportunity on me and extending his grace to complete this book successfully.

I am especially blessed in getting the support of my well-wisher and philosopher, Mrs. Rama Srinivasan, Besant Nagar, Chennai. Without her magnanimous assistance in my academics, I would not have been able to achieve this opportunity. She has been the beacon light in rendering timely moral support.

I am thankful to my colleagues and the students for all their help. I am grateful to my mother Mrs.S.Chandra Swaminathan, wife Mrs.N.Nalini Anbazhagan, sons A.Anish and A.Akhil for having cooperated with me to complete this book. It was the inspiration that I got from them which helped me to mold this work. I thank all my family members, parents-in-law, friends and other well-wishers for their interest in my success.

Finally, I express my sincere thanks to all the CreateSpace members, for his guidance in every step. His significant cooperation and valuable suggestions provided a strong ground for this book. Without his continuous interest and support, this book could not have been completed successfully.

1 BASIC PROGRAMS

1. Program to print the words "My first program in C"

```
#include <stdio.h>

void main()
{
    printf("\nMy first program in C");
}
```

2. Program to print the integer number "143" using variable

```
#include <stdio.h>

void main()
{
    int a;
    a = 143;
    printf("\n%d",a);
}
```

3. Program to read & print the age of the person

```
#include <stdio.h>

void main()
{
    int age;
    printf("\nEnter age: ");
    scanf("%d",&age);
    printf("\nAge is %d",age);
}
```

4. Program to read & print the height of the person

```
#include <stdio.h>
```

```c
void main()
{
    float ht;
    printf("\nEnter height: ");
    scanf("%f",&ht);
    printf("\nHeight is %f",ht);
}
```

5. Program to read & print the mark grade of the "C programming language" subject

```c
#include <stdio.h>

void main()
{
    char grade;
    printf("\nEnter mark grade: ");
    scanf("%c",&grade);
    printf("\nMark grade is %c",grade);
}
```

6. Program to add two numbers

```c
#include <stdio.h>

void main()
{
    double n1, n2, res;
    printf("\nEnter two numbers\n");
    scanf("%lf%lf",&n1,&n2);
    res = n1 + n2;
    printf("\nSum is %lf",res);
}
```

7. Program to calculate the area & circumference of the circle

```c
#include <stdio.h>

#define PI 3.14

void main()
{
    float r, a, c;
    printf("\nEnter radius: ");
    scanf("%f",&r);
    a = PI * r * r;
    c = 2 * PI * r;
    printf("\nRadius is %f",r);
    printf("\nArea is %f\nCircumference is %f",a,c);
}
```

8. Program to calculate the area & perimeter of the rectangle

```c
#include <stdio.h>

void main()
{
    float l, b, a, p;
    printf("\nEnter length: ");
    scanf("%f",&l);
    printf("\nEnter breadth: ");
    scanf("%f",&b);
    a = l * b;
    p = 2 * (l + b);
    printf("\nLength is %f",l);
    printf("\nBreadth is %f",b);
    printf("\nArea is %f\nPerimeter is %f",a,p);
}
```

9. Program to calculate the simple interest

```c
#include <stdio.h>

void main()
{
    float p, n, r, si;
    printf("\nEnter principle amount, number of year and rate of interest\n");
    scanf("%f%f%f",&p,&n,&r);
    si = p * n * r / 100;
    printf("\nPrinciple amount is %f",p);
    printf("\nNumber of year is %f",n);
    printf("\nRate of interest is %f",r);
    printf("\nSimple interest is %f",si);
}
```

10. Program to divide the number 9 and 5 with different methods

```c
#include <stdio.h>

void main()
{
    float res;
    res = 9 / 5;
    printf("\nResult is %f",res);
    res = 9 / 5.0;
    printf("\nResult is %f",res);
    res = 9.0 / 5;
    printf("\nResult is %f",res);
    res = 9.0 / 5.0;
    printf("\nResult is %f",res);
}
```

11. Program to find the last digit of the given integer number

```
#include <stdio.h>

void main()
{
    int n, r;
    printf("Enter number: ");
    r = n % 10;
    printf("\nLast digit is %d",r);
}
```

12. Program to understand all the relational operators

```
#include <stdio.h>

void main()
{
    int a = 24, b = 15, r;
    r = a < b;
    printf("\nA < B is %d",r);
    r = a <= b;
    printf("\nA <= B is %d",r);
    r = a > b;
    printf("\nA > B is %d",r);
    r = a >= b;
    printf("\nA >= B is %d",r);
    r = a == b;
    printf("\nA == B is %d",r);
    r = a != b;
    printf("\nA != B is %d",r);
}
```

13. Program to understand all the logical operators

```
#include <stdio.h>

void main()
{
    int a = 24, b = 15, c = 33, r;
    r = a > b && a > c;
    printf("\nA > B && A > C is %d",r);
    r = a > b || a > c;
    printf("\nA > B || A > C is %d",r);
    r = ! (a > b && a > c);
    printf("\n! (A > B && A > C) is %d",r);
}
```

14. Program to understand the prefix and postfix increment operator

```
#include <stdio.h>
```

```c
void main()
{
    int a, r;
    a = 5;
    r = ++a;
    printf("\nA is %d\nR is %d",a,r);
    a = 5;
    r = a++;
    printf("\nA is %d\nR is %d",a,r);
}
```

15. Program to understand all the bitwise operators

```c
#include <stdio.h>

void main()
{
    int a = 24, b = 15, r;
    r = a & b;
    printf("\nA & B is %d",r);
    r = a | b;
    printf("\nA | B is %d",r);
    r = a ^ b;
    printf("\nA ^ B is %d",r);
    r = a << 1;
    printf("\nA << 1 is %d",r);
    r = b >> 2;
    printf("\nB >> 2 is %d",r);
    r = ~a;
    printf("\n~A is %d",r);
}
```

16. Program to understand all the assignment operators

```c
#include <stdio.h>

void main()
{
    int a = 2, r = a;
    printf("\nR is %d",r);
    r += a;
    printf("\nR is %d",r);
    r -= a;
    printf("\nR is %d",r);
    r = a;
    printf("\nR is %d",r);
    r /= a;
    printf("\nR is %d",r);
    r = 19;
    r %= a;
    printf("\nR is %d",r);
    r <<= a;
    printf("\nR is %d",r);
```

```
        r >>= a;
        printf("\nR is %d",r);
        r ^= a;
        printf("\nR is %d",r);
        r |= a;
        printf("\nR is %d",r);
        r &= a;
        printf("\nR is %d",r);
}
```

17. Program to swap the two numbers

```
#include <stdio.h>

void main()
{
        int a, b, t;
        printf("\nEnter two numbers\n");
        scanf("%d%d",&a,&b);
        printf("\nBefore,\nA is %d\nB is %d",a,b);
        t = a, a = b, b = t;
        printf("\nAfter,\nA is %d\nB is %d",a,b);
}
```

18. Program to swap the two numbers without using temporary variable

```
#include <stdio.h>

void main()
{
        int a, b;
        printf("\nEnter two numbers\n");
        scanf("%d%d",&a,&b);
        printf("\nBefore,\nA is %d\nB is %d",a,b);
        a ^= b ^= a ^= b;
        printf("\nAfter,\nA is %d\nB is %d",a,b);
}
```

19. Program to understand the sizeof operator

```
#include <stdio.h>

void main()
{
        int a;
        float b;
        char c;
        double d;
        printf("\n%d",sizeof(a));
        printf("\n%d",sizeof(b));
        printf("\n%d",sizeof(c));
        printf("\n%d",sizeof(d));
```

```
        printf("\n%d",sizeof(1));
        printf("\n%d",sizeof('1'));
        printf("\n%d",sizeof(1.0));
        printf("\n%d",sizeof(1.0f));
        printf("\n%d",sizeof(char));
        printf("\n%d",sizeof(int));
        printf("\n%d",sizeof(float));
        printf("\n%d",sizeof(double));
        printf("\n%d",sizeof(a+b+c+d));
}
```

20. Program to understand the type casting

```
#include <stdio.h>

void main()
{
    int a = 10, b = 3;
    float r;
    r = a / b;
    printf("\nR is %f",r);
    r = a / (float) b;
    printf("\nR is %f",r);
    r = (float) a / b;
    printf("\nR is %f",r);
}
```

21. Program to understand the operator precedence

```
#include <stdio.h>

void main()
{
    float a = 10, b = 20, c = 30, d = 40, r;
    r = a + b / c + d;
    printf("\nR is %f",r);
    r = (a + b) / c + d;
    printf("\nR is %f",r);
    r = a + b / (c + d);
    printf("\nR is %f",r);
    r = (a + b) / (c + d);
    printf("\nR is %f",r);
}
```

22. Program to convert temperature in Celsius to Fahrenheit

```
#include <stdio.h>

void main()
{
    float c, f;
    printf("\nEnter temperature in Celsius: ");
```

```
    scanf("%f",&c);
    f = 9 / 5.0 * c + 32;
    printf("\nTemperature in Fahrenheit is %f",f);
}
```

23. Program to convert temperature in Fahrenheit to Celsius

```
#include <stdio.h>

void main()
{
    float c, f;
    printf("\nEnter temperature in Fahrenheit: ");
    scanf("%f",&f);
    c = 5 / 9.0 * (f - 32);
    printf("\nTemperature in Celsius is %f",c);
}
```

24. Program to find the square root of the given number

```
#include <stdio.h>
#include <math.h>

void main()
{
    double n, r;
    printf("\nEnter number: ");
    scanf("%lf",&n);
    r = sqrt(n);
    printf("\nSquare root of %lf is %lf",n,r);
}
```

25. Program to find the sine, cosine and tangent of the given number

```
#include <stdio.h>
#include <math.h>

#define PI 3.14

void main()
{
    double n, r;
    printf("\nEnter number: ");
    scanf("%lf",&n);
    n = n * PI / 180;
    r = sin(n);
    printf("\nSine value is %lf",r);
    r = cos(n);
    printf("\nCosine value is %lf",r);
    r = tan(n);
    printf("\nTangent value is %lf",r);
}
```

26. Program to find the base of natural logarithm and logarithm base 10

```
#include <stdio.h>
#include <math.h>

void main()
{
    double n, r;
    printf("\nEnter number: ");
    scanf("%lf",&n);
    r = log(n);
    printf("\nNatural logarithm value is %lf",r);
    r = log10(n);
    printf("\nLogarithm base 10 value is %lf",r);
}
```

27. Program to calculate the compound interest

```
#include <stdio.h>
#include <math.h>

void main()
{
    float p, n, r, ci;
    printf("\nEnter principle amount, number of year and rate of interest\n");
    scanf("%f%f%f",&p,&n,&r);
    ci = p * pow(1 + r / 100,n);
    printf("\nPrinciple amount is %f",p);
    printf("\nNumber of year is %f",n);
    printf("\nRate of interest is %f",r);
    printf("\nCompound interest is %f",ci);
}
```

28. Program to calculate the area & volume of the cylinder

```
#include <stdio.h>

#define PI 3.14

void main()
{
    float r, h, a, v;
    printf("\nEnter radius: ");
    scanf("%f",&r);
    printf("\nEnter height: ");
    scanf("%f",&h);
    a = 2 * PI * r * (r + h);
    v = PI * r * r * h;
    printf("\nArea is %f\nVolume is %f",a,v);
}
```

2 CONTROL / DECISION MAKING PROGRAMS

1. Program to find the largest of two numbers using "simple if"

```c
#include <stdio.h>

void main()
{
    int a, b, m;
    printf("\nEnter two numbers\n");
    scanf("%d%d",&a,&b);
    m = a;
    if(b > a)
    {
        m = b;
    }
    printf("\nLargest number is %d",m);
}
```

2. Program to find the largest of two numbers using "if...else"

```c
#include <stdio.h>

void main()
{
    int a, b, m;
    printf("\nEnter two numbers\n");
    scanf("%d%d",&a,&b);
    scanf("%d",&b);
    if(a > b)
    {
        m = a;
    }
    else
    {
        m = b;
    }
    printf("\nLargest number is %d",m);
}
```

3. Program to find the largest of two numbers using conditional operator

```c
#include <stdio.h>

void main()
{
    int a, b, m;
    printf("\nEnter two numbers\n");
    scanf("%d%d",&a,&b);
    m = a > b ? a : b;
    printf("\nLargest number is %d",m);
}
```

4. Program to find the largest of three numbers using "nested if...else"

```c
#include <stdio.h>

void main()
{
    int a, b, c, m;
    printf("\nEnter three numbers\n");
    scanf("%d%d%d",&a,&b,&c);
    if(a > b)
    {
        if(a > c)
        {
            m = a;
        }
        else
        {
            m = c;
        }
    }
    else
    {
        if(b > c)
        {
            m = b;
        }
        else
        {
            m = c;
        }
    }
    printf("\nLargest number is %d",m);
}
```

5. Program to find the largest of three numbers using conditional operator

```c
#include <stdio.h>
```

```
void main()
{
    int a, b, c, m;
    printf("\nEnter three numbers\n");
    scanf("%d%d%d",&a,&b,&c);
    m = a > b ? (a > c ? a : c) : (b > c ? b : c);
    printf("\nLargest number is %d",m);
}
```

6. Program to find the number of digits using "string of if...else / else...if ladder"

```
#include <stdio.h>

void main()
{
    int n;
    printf("\nEnter number: ");
    scanf("%d",&n);
    if(n <= 9)
        printf("\nSingle digit number");
    else if(n <= 99)
        printf("\nDouble digit number");
    else if(n <= 999)
        printf("\nTriple digit number");
    else
        printf("\nMore than three digit number");
}
```

7. Program to do four function calculator based on the user choice using "switch...case"

```
#include <stdio.h>

void main()
{
    int a, b, res, opt;
    printf("\nEnter two numbers\n");
    scanf("%d%d",&a,&b);
    printf("\n1. Add two numbers");
    printf("\n2. Subtract two numbers");
    printf("\n3. Multiply two numbers");
    printf("\n4. Divide two numbers");
    printf("\n\nEnter option: ");
    scanf("%d",&opt);
    switch(opt)
    {
        case 1:
            res = a + b;
            break;
        case 2:
            res = a - b;
            break;
```

```
        case 3:
              res = a * b;
              break;
        case 4:
              res = a / b;
              break;
        default:
              printf("\nInvalid option");
              return;
    }
    printf("\nResult is %d",res);
}
```

8. Program to find whether the number is odd or even

/* Method 1 */

```
#include <stdio.h>

void main()
{
    int n;
    printf("\nEnter number: ");
    scanf("%d",&n);
    if(n % 2 == 0)
    {
        printf("\nEven number");
    }
    else
    {
        printf("\nOdd number");
    }
}
```

/* Method 2 */

```
#include <stdio.h>

void main()
{
    int n;
    printf("\nEnter number: ");
    scanf("%d",&n);
    if(n % 2)
    {
        printf("\nOdd number");
    }
    else
    {
        printf("\nEven number");
    }
}
```

```
/* Method 3 */

#include <stdio.h>

void main()
{
    int n;
    printf("\nEnter number: ");
    scanf("%d",&n);
    if(n & 1)
        printf("\nOdd number");
    else
        printf("\nEven number");
}

/* Method 4 */

#include <stdio.h>

void main()
{
    int n;
    printf("\nEnter number: ");
    scanf("%d",&n);
    n % 2 ? printf("\nOdd") : printf("\nEven");
}
```

9. Program to find whether the year is leap or non leap

```
#include <stdio.h>

void main()
{
    int n;
    printf("\nEnter year: ");
    scanf("%d",&n);
    if( (n%4 == 0 && year%100 != 0) || year%100 == 0 )
        printf("\nLeap year");
    else
        printf("\nNon leap year");
}
```

10. Program to find whether the number is positive or negative

```
#include <stdio.h>

void main()
{
    int n;
    printf("\nEnter number: ");
    scanf("%d",&n);
    n >= 0 ? printf("\nPositive number") :  printf("\nNegative number");
}
```

11. Program to calculate the electricity bill amount based on the following conditions

Units	Amount
0-100	0.75 rupees
101-200	1.5 rupees
201-500	3 rupees
> 500	5 rupees

```c
#include <stdio.h>

void main()
{
    int u;
    float a;
    printf("\nEnter number of units consumed: ");
    scanf("%d",&u);
    if(u <= 100)
        a = u * 0.75;
    else if(u <= 200)
        a = 75 + (u - 100) * 1.5;
    else if(u <= 500)
        a = 75 + 150 + (u - 200) * 3;
    else
        a = 75 + 150 + 900 + (u - 500) * 5;
    printf("\nAmount paid to EB is %.2f",a);
}
```

12. Program to do trigonometry calculations based on the user choice

```c
#include <stdio.h>
#include <math.h>

#define PI 3.14

void main()
{
    double n,a;
    int opt;
    printf("\nEnter number: ");
    scanf("%lf",&n);
    printf("\n1. To calculate sine");
    printf("\n2. To calculate cosine");
    printf("\n3. To calculate tangent");
    printf("\nEnter option: ");
    scanf("%d",&opt);
    n = n * PI / 180;
    switch(opt)
    {
        case 1:
            a = sin(n);
            break;
        case 2:
            a = cos(n);
            break;
```

```
            case 3:
                a = tan(n);
                break;
            default:
                printf("\nInvalid option");
                return;
        }
        printf("\nResult is %lf",a);
}
```

13. Program to solve the quadratic equation

```
#include<stdio.h>
#include<math.h>

void main()
{
    float a, b, c, d, r1, r2;
    printf("\nEnter a, b and c coefficient values\n");
    scanf("%f%f%f",&a,&b,&c);
    d = (b * b) - (4 * a * c);
    if(d == 0)
    {
        printf("\nRoots are real and equal");
        r1 = -b / (2 * a);
        r2 = r1;
        printf("\nRoot 1 = %f",r1);
        printf("\nRoot 2 = %f",r2);
    }
    else if(d > 0)
    {
        printf("\nRoots are real and unequal");
        r1 = (-b + sqrt(d)) / (2 * a);
        r2 = (-b - sqrt(d)) / (2 * a);
        printf("\nRoot 1 = %f",r1);
        printf("\nRoot 2 = %f",r2);
    }
    else
    {
        printf("\nRoots are imaginary and unequal");
        r1 = -b / (2 * a);
        r2 = sqrt(-d) / (2 * a);
        printf("\nRoot 1 = %f+%fi",r1,r2);
        printf("\nRoot 2 = %f-%fi",r1,r2);
    }
}
```

14. Program to convert upper to lower case character

```
#include <stdio.h>
```

```c
void main()
{
    char c;
    printf("\nEnter character: ");
    scanf("%c",&c);
    if(c >= 'A' && c <= 'Z')
        c = c + 32;
    printf("\nNow, character is %c",c);
}
```

15. Program to convert lower to upper case character

/* Method 1 */

```c
#include <stdio.h>
#include <ctype.h>

void main()
{
    char c;
    printf("\nEnter character: ");
    c = getchar();
    if(islower(c))
        c = toupper(c);
    printf("\nNow, character is %c",c);
}
```

/* Method 2 */

```c
#include <stdio.h>
#include <ctype.h>

void main()
{
    char c;
    printf("\nEnter character: ");
    c = getchar();
    c = toupper(c);
    printf("\nNow, character is %c",c);
}
```

16. Program to display whether the character is alphabet, digit or special symbol

```c
#include <stdio.h>
#include <ctype.h>

void main()
{
    char c;
    printf("\nEnter character: ");
    c = getchar();
    if(isalpha(c))
        printf("\nAlphabet");
```

```
        else if(isdigit(c))
              printf("\nDigit");
        else
              printf("\nSpecial symbol");
}
```

17. Program to display whether the number is divisible by 6

```
#include <stdio.h>

void main()
{
      int n;
      printf("\nEnter number: ");
      scanf("%d",&n);
      if(n%6 == 0)
            printf("\n%d is divisible by 6",n);
      else
            printf("\n%d is not divisible by 6",n);
}
```

18. Program to print the following word line by line C, C++, Java and C# except Java

```
#include <stdio.h>

void main()
{
      printf("\nC");
      printf("\nC++");
      goto forward;
      printf("\nJava");
      forward:
      printf("\nC#");
}
```

19. Program to print the word Java repeatedly for ten times

```
#include <stdio.h>

void main()
{
      int n;
      n = 1;
      back:
      n++;
      printf("\nJava");
      if(n <= 10)
            goto back;
}
```

3 LOOP / ITERATIVE PROGRAMS

1. Program to print the name Dennis M. Ritchie repeatedly for ten times using "while"

```
#include <stdio.h>

void main()
{
    int n;
    n = 1;
    while(n <= 10)
    {
        printf("\nDennis M. Ritchie");
        n++;
    }
}
```

2. Program to print the name Brian W. Kernighan repeatedly for ten times using "for"

```
#include <stdio.h>

void main()
{
    int n;
    for(n = 1;n <= 10;n++)
        printf("\nBrian W. Kernighan");
}
```

3. Program to read & print the subject mark (Note: The mark is between 0 and 100)

```
#include <stdio.h>

void main()
{
    int mark;
    do
    {
        printf("\nEnter mark: ");
```

```
        scanf("%d",&mark);
    }
    while(mark < 0 || mark > 100);
    printf("\nMark is %d",mark);
}
```

4. Program to print the first 15 natural numbers

```
#include <stdio.h>

void main()
{
    int n;
    for(n = 1;n <= 15;n++)
        printf("\n%d",n);
}
```

5. Program to print the first "n" natural numbers

```
#include <stdio.h>

void main()
{
    int n, i;
    printf("\nEnter n value: ");
    scanf("%d",&n);
    for(i = 1;i <= n;i++)
        printf("\n%d",i);
}
```

6. Program to calculate the sum = 1 + 2 + 3 + ... + n

```
#include <stdio.h>

void main()
{
    int n, i, sum = 0;
    printf("\nEnter n value: ");
    scanf("%d",&n);
    for(i = 1;i <= n;i++)
        sum += i;
    printf("\nSum = %d",sum);
}
```

7. Program to calculate the sum = 1 + 3 + 5 + ... + n

```
#include <stdio.h>

void main()
{
    int n, i, sum = 0;
```

```c
    printf("\nEnter n value: ");
    scanf("%d",&n);
    for(i = 1;i <= n;i+=2)
        sum += i;
    printf("\nSum = %d",sum);
}
```

8. Program to calculate the sum = 2 + 4 + 6 + ... + n

```c
#include <stdio.h>

void main()
{
    int n, i, sum = 0;

    printf("\nEnter n value: ");
    scanf("%d",&n);
    for(i = 2;i <= n;i+=2)
        sum += i;
    printf("\nSum = %d",sum);
}
```

9. Program to generate the Fibonacci series

```c
#include <stdio.h>

void main()
{
    int n, i, f1 = -1, f2 = 1, f3;
    printf("\nEnter number of series generate: ");
    scanf("%d",&n);
    for(i = 1;i <= n;i++)
    {
        f3 = f1 + f2;
        printf("%d ",f3);
        f1 = f2;
        f2 = f3;
    }
}
```

10. Program to find the factorial value

```c
#include <stdio.h>

void main() {
    int n, i, f = 1;
    printf("\nEnter n value: ");
    scanf("%d",&n);
    for(i = 1;i <= n;i++)
        f *= i;
    printf("\nFactorial of %d is %d",n,f);
}
```

11. Program to find the x^n value

```c
#include <stdio.h>

void main()
{
    float x, r = 1;
    int n, i;
    printf("\nEnter x value: ");
    scanf("%f",&x);
    printf("\nEnter n value: ");
    scanf("%d",&n);
    for(i = 1;i <= n;i++)
        r *= x;
    printf("\n%f to the power %d is %f",x,n,r);
}
```

12. Program to find the sum of digits

```c
#include <stdio.h>

void main()
{
    int n, r, s = 0;
    printf("\nEnter number: ");
    scanf("%d",&n);
    while(n != 0)
    {
        r = n % 10;
        s += r;
        n /= 10;
    }
    printf("\nSum of digit is %d",s);
}
```

13. Program to reverse the number

```c
#include <stdio.h>

void main()
{
    int n, r;
    printf("\nEnter number: ");
    scanf("%d",&n);
    printf("\nReversed number is ");
    while(n != 0)
    {
        r = n % 10;
        printf("%d",r);
        n /= 10;
    }
}
```

14. Program to find whether the number is Armstrong or not a Armstrong

```c
#include <stdio.h>

void main()
{
    int n, x, r, s = 0;
    printf("\nEnter number: ");
    scanf("%d",&n);
    x = n;
    while(n != 0)
    {
        r = n % 10;
        s += r * r * r;
        n /= 10;
    }
    if(s == x)
        printf("\nThe number is Armstrong");
    else
        printf("\nThe number is not a Armstrong");

}
```

15. Program to understand the "break"

```c
#include <stdio.h>

void main()
{
    int n;
    for(n = 1;n <= 15;n++)
    {
        if(i == 10)
            break;
        printf("\n%d",n);
    }
}
```

16. Program to understand the "continue"

```c
#include <stdio.h>

void main()
{
    int n;
    for(n = 1;n <= 15;n++)
    {
        if(i%3 == 0)
            continue;
        printf("\n%d",n);
    }
}
```

17. Program to find whether the number is prime or not

```
#include <stdio.h>

void main()
{
    int n, i;
    printf("\nEnter n value: ");
    scanf("%d",&n);
    for(i = 2;i < n;i++)
    {
        if(n%i == 0)
            break;
    }
    if(i == n)
        printf("\nPrime");
    else
        printf("\nNot a prime");
}
```

18. Program to find the square root of the given number till the user gives -1

```
#include <stdio.h>
#include <math.h>

void main()
{
    float ans, n;
    do
    {
        printf("\nGive number: ");
        scanf("%f",&n);
        if(n < 0)
            continue;
        ans = sqrt(n);
        printf("\nSquare root of %f is %f",n,ans);
    }
    while(n != -1);
}
```

19. Program to calculate the sin(x) series

```
#include <stdio.h>

#define PI 3.14

void main()
{
    float x, nr, dr, r = 0;
    int sign, i;
    printf("\nEnter x value: ");
    scanf("%f",&x);
    x = x * PI / 180;
```

```
        for(nr = x, dr = 1, sign = 1, i = 2; 1 ; i++)
        {
            r = r + (nr / dr) * sign;
            sign = - sign;
            nr = nr * x * x;
            dr = dr * i;
            i++;
            dr = dr * i;
            if(nr/dr < 0.000001)
                break;
        }
        printf("\nsin(%f) = %f",x,r);
}
```

20. Program to calculate the cos(x) series

```
#include <stdio.h>

#define PI 3.14

void main()
{
    float x, nr, dr, r = 0;
    int sign, i;
    printf("\nEnter x value: ");
    scanf("%f",&x);
    x = x * PI / 180;
    for(nr = 1, dr = 1, sign = 1, i = 1; 1 ; i++)
    {
        r = r + (nr / dr) * sign;
        sign = - sign;
        nr = nr * x * x;
        dr = dr * i;
        i++;
        dr = dr * i;
        if(nr/dr < 0.000001)
            break;
    }
    printf("\ncos(%f) = %f",x,r);
}
```

21. Program to calculate the e^x series

```
#include <stdio.h>

void main()
{
    float x, nr, dr, r = 1;
    int i;
    printf("\nEnter x value: ");
    scanf("%f",&x);
```

```
        for(nr = x, dr = 1, i = 2; 1 ; i++)
        {
                r = r + nr / dr;
                nr = nr * x;
                dr = dr * i;
                if(nr/dr < 0.000001)
                        break;
        }
        printf("\nexp(%f) = %f",x,r);
}
```

22. Program to calculate the sinh(x) series

```
#include <stdio.h>

#define PI 3.14

void main()
{
        float x, nr, dr, r = 0;
        int i;
        printf("\nEnter x value: ");
        scanf("%f",&x);
        x = x * PI / 180;
        for(nr = x, dr = 1, i = 2; 1 ; i++)
        {
                r = r + nr / dr;
                nr = nr * x * x;
                dr = dr * i;
                i++;
                dr = dr * i;
                if(nr/dr < 0.000001)
                        break;
        }
        printf("\nsinh(%f) = %f",x,r);
}
```

23. Program to calculate the cosh(x) series

```
#include <stdio.h>

#define PI 3.14

void main()
{
        float x, nr, dr, r = 0;
        int sign, i;
        printf("\nEnter x value: ");
        scanf("%f",&x);
        x = x * PI / 180;
        for(nr = 1, dr = 1, i = 1; 1 ; i++)
        {
                r = r + nr / dr;
```

```
            nr = nr * x * x;
            dr = dr * i;
            i++;
            dr = dr * i;
            if(nr/dr < 0.000001)
                    break;
    }
    printf("\ncosh(%f) = %f",x,r);
}
```

24. Program to show the multiplication table

```
#include <stdio.h>

void main()
{
    int x, n, i;
    printf("\nEnter which table: ");
    scanf("%d",&x);
    printf("\nEnter upto which: ");
    scanf("%d",&n);
    for(i = 1;i <= n;i++)
        printf("\n%d * %d = %d",i,x,i*x);
}
```

25. Program to understand the "nested loops"

```
#include <stdio.h>

void main()
{
    int i, j;
    for(i = 1;i <= 5;i++)
    {
        printf("\n");
        for(j = 1;j <= 5;j++)
        {
            printf("(%d,%d)",i,j);
        }
    }
}
```

26. Program to print the following sequence

```
    1
    1   2
    1   2   3
    1   2   3   4
    ...
```

```
#include <stdio.h>
```

```c
void main()
{
    int n, i, j;
    printf("\nEnter n value: ");
    scanf("%d",&n);
    for(i = 1;i <= n;i++)
    {
        printf("\n");
        for(j = 1;j <= i;j++)
        {
            printf("%d\t",j);
        }
    }
}
```

27. Program to print the following sequence

```
1
2   2
3   3   3
4   4   4   4
...
```

```c
#include <stdio.h>

void main()
{
    int n, i, j;
    printf("\nEnter n value: ");
    scanf("%d",&n);
    for(i = 1;i <= n;i++)
    {
        printf("\n");
        for(j = 1;j <= i;j++)
        {
            printf("%d\t",i);
        }
    }
}
```

28. Program to print the following sequence

```
1
0   0
1   1   1
0   0   0   0
...
```

```c
#include <stdio.h>

void main()
{
    int n, i, j;
    printf("\nEnter n value: ");
    scanf("%d",&n);
```

```
        for(i = 1;i <= n;i++)
        {
            printf("\n");
            for(j = 1;j <= i;j++)
            {
                printf("%d\t",i%2 == 0 ? 0 : 1);
            }
        }
}
```

29. Program to print the following sequence
```
    1
    1   0
    1   0   1
    1   0   1   0
    ...
```

```
#include <stdio.h>

void main()
{
    int n, i, j;
    printf("\nEnter n value: ");
    scanf("%d",&n);
    for(i = 1;i <= n;i++)
    {
        printf("\n");
        for(j = 1;j <= i;j++)
        {
            printf("%d\t",j%2 == 0 ? 0 : 1);
        }
    }
}
```

30. Program to print the following sequence
```
    *
    *   *
    *   *   *
    *   *   *   *
    ...
```

```
#include <stdio.h>

void main() {
    int n, i, j;
    printf("\nEnter n value: ");
    scanf("%d",&n);
    for(i = 1;i <= n;i++) {
        printf("\n");
        for(j = 1;j <= i;j++)
            printf("*\t");
    }
}
```

31. Program to print the following sequence

```
...
*    *    *    *
*    *    *
*    *
*
```

```c
#include <stdio.h>

void main()
{
    int n, i, j;
    printf("\nEnter n value: ");
    scanf("%d",&n);
    for(i = n;i >= 1;i--)
    {
        printf("\n");
        for(j = 1;j <= i;j++)
            printf("*\t");
    }
}
```

32. Program to print the following sequence

```
            *
        *    *
    *    *    *
*    *    *    *
...
```

```c
#include <stdio.h>

void main()
{
    int n, i, j;
    printf("\nEnter n value: ");
    scanf("%d",&n);
    for(i = 1;i <= n;i++)
    {
        printf("\n");
        for(j = 1;j <= n – i;j++)
            printf("\t");
        for(j = 1;j <= i;j++)
            printf("*\t");
    }
}
```

33. Program to print the following sequence

```
            *
        *    *    *
    *    *    *    *    *
*    *    *    *    *    *    *
...
```

```c
#include <stdio.h>

void main()
{
    int n, i, j;
    printf("\nEnter n value: ");
    scanf("%d",&n);
    for(i = 1;i <= n;i++)
    {
        printf("\n");
        for(j = 1;j <= n – i;j++)
            printf(" ");
        for(j = 1;j <= 2 * i - 1;j++)
            printf("* ");
    }
}
```

34. Program to find prime numbers between the specified range

```c
#include <stdio.h>

void main()
{
    int n1, n2, i, n;
    printf("\nEnter range start value: ");
    scanf("%d",&n1);
    printf("\nEnter range end value: ");
    scanf("%d",&n2);
    printf("\nThe prime numbers between %d and %d are\n",n1,n2);
    for(n = n1;n <= n2;n++)
    {
        for(i = 2;i < n;i++)
        {
            if(n%i == 0)
                break;
        }
        if(i == n)
            printf("%d ",n);
    }
}
```

35. Program to do four function calculator based on the user choice using loop

```c
#include <stdio.h>
void main()
{
    int a, b, res, opt;
    do
    {
        printf("\nEnter two numbers\n");
        scanf("%d%d",&a,&b);
        printf("\n1. Add two numbers");
        printf("\n2. Subtract two numbers");
```

```
            printf("\n3. Multiply two numbers");
            printf("\n4. Divide two numbers");
            printf("\n5. Exit");
            printf("\n\nEnter option: ");
            scanf("%d",&opt);
            switch(opt)
            {
                case 1:
                    res = a + b;
                    break;
                case 2:
                    res = a - b;
                    break;
                case 3:
                    res = a * b;
                    break;
                case 4:
                    res = a / b;
                    break;
                default:
                    printf("\nInvalid option");
            }
            printf("\nResult is %d",res);
    }
    while(opt != 5);
}
```

36. Program to read the five numbers & print the same

```
#include <stdio.h>

void main()
{
    int n1, n2, n3, n4, n5;
    printf("\nEnter five numbers\n");
    scanf("%d%d%d%d%d",&n1,&n2,&n3,&n4,&n5);
    printf("\nNumber 1 = %d",n1);
    printf("\nNumber 1 = %d",n2);
    printf("\nNumber 1 = %d",n3);
    printf("\nNumber 1 = %d",n4);
    printf("\nNumber 1 = %d",n5);
}
```

4 ARRAY PROGRAMS

1. Program to initialize & print the array elements

```c
#include <stdio.h>

void main()
{
    int n[5] = {12,34,56,78,90}, i;
    for(i = 0;i < 5;i++)
        printf("\nElement %d = %d",i+1,n[i]);
}
```

2. Program to read the five numbers & print the same using array

```c
#include <stdio.h>

void main()
{
    int n[5], i;
    printf("\nEnter five numbers\n");
    for(i = 0;i < 5;i++)
        scanf("%d",&n[i]);
    for(i = 0;i < 5;i++)
        printf("\nElement %d = %d",i+1,n[i]);
}
```

3. Program to find the sum & average of 'n' different numbers

```c
#include <stdio.h>

void main()
{
    float x[50], sum = 0, avg;
    int n, i;
    printf("\nEnter how many number(s): ");
    scanf("%d",&n);
    printf("\nEnter %d number(s)\n",n);
```

```
for(i = 0;i < n;i++)
{
        scanf("%f",&x[i]);
        sum += x[i];
}
avg = sum / n;
printf("\nSum = %f",sum);
printf("\nAverage = %f",avg);
}
```

4. Program to find the small & large of 'n' different numbers

```
#include <stdio.h>

void main()
{
        float x[50], s, l;
        int n, i;
        printf("\nEnter how many number(s): ");
        scanf("%d",&n);
        printf("\nEnter %d number(s)\n",n);
        for(i = 0;i < n;i++)
                scanf("%f",&x[i]);
        s = l = x[0];
        for(i = 0;i < n;i++)
        {
                if(x[i] > l)
                        l = x[i];
                if(x[i] < s)
                        s = x[i];
        }
        printf("\nSmall number from the list is = %f",s);
        printf("\nLarge number from the list is = %f",l);
}
```

5. Program to find the mean, variance and standard deviation

```
#include <stdio.h>
#include <math.h>

void main()
{
        float x[50], stddev, sum = 0, mean, variance;
        int n, i;
        printf("\nEnter how many number(s): ");
        scanf("%d",&n);
        printf("\nEnter %d number(s)\n",n);
        for(i = 0;i < n;i++)
        {
                scanf("%f",&x[i]);
                sum += x[i];
        }
        mean = sum / n;
```

```
        for(i = 0, sum = 0;i < n;i++)
                sum += pow(x[i] – mean, 2.0);
        variance = sum / n;
        stddev = sqrt(variance);
        printf("\nMean = %f",mean);
        printf("\nVariance = %f",variance);
        printf("\nStandard deviation = %f",stddev);
}
```

6. Program to print the find the element from the list

```
#include <stdio.h>

void main()
{
        float x[50], f;
        int n, i;
        printf("\nEnter number of element(s): ");
        scanf("%d",&n);
        printf("\nEnter %d number(s)\n",n);
        for(i = 0;i < n;i++)
                scanf("%f",&x[i]);
        printf("\nEnter the number to find: ");
        scanf("%f",&f);
        for(i = 0;i < n;i++)
        {
            if(x[i] == f)
            {
                    printf("\n%f is found at %d",f,i+1);
                    break;
            }
        }
        if(i == n)
                printf("\n%f is not found",f);
}
```

7. Program to initialize & print the string

```
#include <stdio.h>

void main()
{
        char name[30] = "Dennis M. Ritchie";
        printf("\nNow, the string contains %s",name);
}
```

8. Program to read & print the string

```
/* Method 1 */
```

```
#include <stdio.h>

void main()
{
    char name[30];
    printf("\nEnter name\n");
    scanf("%s",name);
    printf("\nNow, the string contains %s",name);
}
```

/* Method 2 */

```
#include <stdio.h>

void main()
{
    char name[30];
    printf("\nEnter name\n");
    gets(name);
    printf("\nNow, the string contains %s",name);
}
```

/* Method 3 */

```
#include <stdio.h>

void main()
{
    char name[30];
    printf("\nEnter name\n");
    scanf("%[^\n]",name);
    printf("\nNow, the string contains %s",name);
}
```

9. Program to copy the string

```
#include <stdio.h>
#include <string.h>

void main()
{
    char str1[30], str2[30], str3[30];
    int i;
    printf("\nEnter string to copy\n");
    gets(str1);
    for(i = 0;str1[i] != '\0';i++)
        str2[i] = str1[i];
    str2[i] = '\0';
    strcpy(str3,str1);
    printf("\nCopied string (w/o fun) is %s",str2);
    printf("\nCopied string (with fun) is %s",str3);
}
```

10. Program to appends one string to another

/* Method 1 (without using function) */

```c
#include <stdio.h>

void main()
{
    char str1[30], str2[30];
    int i, j;
    printf("\nEnter string 1\n");
    gets(str1);
    printf("\nEnter string 2\n");
    gets(str2);
    printf("\nString 1 is %s",str1);
    printf("\nString 2 is %s",str2);
    for(i = 0;str1[i] != '\0';i++);
    for(j = 0;str2[j] != '\0';j++, i++)
            str1[i] = str2[j];
    str1[i] = '\0';
    printf("\nNow, string 1 is %s",str1);
    printf("\nNow, string 2 is %s",str2);
}
```

/* Method 2 (with using function) */

```c
#include <stdio.h>
#include <string.h>

void main()
{
    char str1[30], str2[30];
    printf("\nEnter string 1\n");
    gets(str1);

    printf("\nEnter string 2\n");
    gets(str2);
    printf("\nString 1 is %s",str1);
    printf("\nString 2 is %s",str2);
    strcat(str1,str2);
    printf("\nNow, string 1 is %s",str1);
    printf("\nNow, string 2 is %s",str2);
}
```

11. Program to count the number of characters in a given string

```c
#include <stdio.h>
#include <string.h>

void main()
{
    char str[30];
    int i, n;
```

```
        printf("\nEnter string\n");
        gets(str);
        for(i = 0;str[i] != '\0';i++);
        n = strlen(str);
        printf("\nString length (w/o fun) is %d",i);
        printf("\nString length (with fun) is %d",n);
}
```

12. Program to compare the two strings

```
#include <stdio.h>
#include <string.h>

void main()
{
        char str1[30], str2[30];
        int n;
        printf("\nEnter string 1\n");
        scanf("%s",str1);
        printf("\nEnter string 2\n");
        scanf("%s",str2);
        n = strcmp(str1,str2);
        if(n == 0)
                printf("\nString 1 = String 2");
        else if(n > 0)
                printf("\nString 1 > String 2");
        else
                printf("\nString 1 < String 2");
}
```

13. Program to do some string manipulation functions

```
#include <stdio.h>
#include <string.h>

void main()
{
        char str[30];
        printf("\nEnter string\n");
        gets(str);

        printf("\nUpper case string is %s",strupr(str));
        printf("\nLower case string is %s",strlwr(str));
        printf("\nReverse string is %s",strrev(str));
}
```

14. Program to reverse the given string

```
/* Method 1 (without using function) */
```

```c
#include <stdio.h>

void main()
{
    char str[30], t;
    int i, n;
    printf("\nEnter string\n");
    gets(str);
    for(n = 0;str[n] != '\0';n++);
    for(i = 0;i < n / 2;i++)
    {
        t = str[i];
        str[i] = str[n - i - 1];
        str[n - i - 1] = t;
    }
    printf("\nReverse string is %s",str);
}
```

/* Method 2 (without using function) */

```c
#include <stdio.h>

void main()
{
    char str[30], revstr[30];
    int i, n;
    printf("\nEnter string\n");
    gets(str);
    for(n = 0;str[n] != '\0';n++);
    for(i = 0;i < n ;i++)
            revstr[i] = str[n - i - 1];
    revstr[i] = '\0';
    printf("\nReverse string is %s",revstr);
}
```

15. Program to find the palindrome string

```c
#include <stdio.h>
#include <string.h>

void main()
{
    char str[30], revstr[30];
    printf("\nEnter string\n");
    gets(str);
    strcpy(revstr,str);
    strrev(revstr);
    if(stricmp(str,revstr) == 0)
            printf("\n%s string is palindrome",str);
    else
            printf("\n%s string is not a palindrome",str);
}
```

16. Program to count the number of alphabets, numerals, and special symbols in a given string

```
#include <stdio.h>
#include <ctype.h>
#include <string.h>

void main()
{
    char str[100];
    int i, na = 0, nn = 0, ns1 = 0, ns2 = 0;
    printf("\nEnter string\n");
    gets(str);
    for(i = 0;i < strlen(str);i++)
    {
        if(isalpha(str[i]))
            na++;
        else if(isdigit(str[i]))
            nn++;
        else if(isspace(str[i]))
            ns1++;
        else
            ns2++;
    }
    printf("\nNumber of alphabets: %d",na);
    printf("\nNumber of numerals: %d",nn);
    printf("\nNumber of space characters: %d",ns1);
    printf("\nNumber of special symbols: %d",ns2);
}
```

17. Program to find the number of occurrence of the character in a string

```
#include <stdio.h>

void main()
{
    char str[100], c;
    int i ,n = 0;
    printf("\nEnter string\n");
    gets(str);
    printf("\nEnter the character to find: ");
    scanf("%c",&c);
    for(i = 0;str[i] != '\0';i++)
        if(str[i] == c)
            n++;
    printf("\nNumber of occurrence of %c is %d",c,n);
}
```

18. Program to understand the two dimensional array

```
#include <stdio.h>
```

```
void main()
{
    int x[3][3] = { {1,2,3}, {4,5,6}, {7,8,9} }, i, j;
    for(i = 0;i < 3;i++)
    {
        printf("\n");
        for(j = 0;j < 3;j++)
            printf("%d\t",x[i][j]);
    }
}
```

19. Program to read & print the specified number of rows and column matrix

```
#include <stdio.h>

void main()
{
    int x[10][10], i, j, r, c;
    printf("\nEnter number of rows and columns\n");
    scanf("%d%d",&r,&c);
    printf("\nEnter %dx%d matrix values\n",r,c);
    for(i = 0;i < r;i++)
        for(j = 0;j < c;j++)
            scanf("%d",&x[i][j]);
    printf("\nGiven matrix is\n");
    for(i = 0;i < r;i++)
    {
        printf("\n");
        for(j = 0;j < c;j++)
            printf("%d\t",x[i][j]);
    }
}
```

20. Program to add two matrices

```
#include <stdio.h>

void main()
{
    int x[10][10], y[10][10], z[10][10], i, j, r, c;
    printf("Enter number of rows and columns\n");
    scanf("%d%d",&r,&c);
    printf("\nEnter %dx%d matrix 1 values\n",r,c);
    for(i = 0;i < r;i++)
        for(j = 0;j < c;j++)
            scanf("%d",&x[i][j]);
    printf("\nEnter %dx%d matrix 2 values\n",r,c);
    for(i = 0;i < r;i++) {
        for(j = 0;j < c;j++) {
            scanf("%d",&y[i][j]);
            z[i][j] = x[i][j] + y[i][j];
        }
    }
}
```

```
printf("\n\nGiven matrix 1 is\n");
for(i = 0;i < r;i++)
{
    printf("\n");
    for(j = 0;j < c;j++)
        printf("%d\t",x[i][j]);
}
printf("\n\nGiven matrix 2 is\n");
for(i = 0;i < r;i++)
{
    printf("\n");
    for(j = 0;j < c;j++)
        printf("%d\t",y[i][j]);
}

printf("\n\nResultant matrix is\n");
for(i = 0;i < r;i++)
{
    printf("\n");
    for(j = 0;j < c;j++)
        printf("%d\t",z[i][j]);
}
}
```

21. Program to multiply two matrices

```
#include <stdio.h>

void main()
{
    int x[10][10], y[10][10], z[10][10];
    int i, j, k, r1, c1, r2, c2;
    printf("Enter matix 1 rows and columns\n");
    scanf("%d%d",&r1,&c1);
    printf("Enter matix 2 rows and columns\n");
    scanf("%d%d",&r2,&c2);
    if(c1 != r2)
    {
        printf("\nMarix can't be multiplied");
        return;
    }
    printf("\nEnter %dx%d matrix 1 values\n",r1,c1);
    for(i = 0;i < r1;i++)
        for(j = 0;j < c1;j++)
            scanf("%d",&x[i][j]);
    printf("\nEnter %dx%d matrix 2 values\n",r2,c2);
    for(i = 0;i < r2;i++)
        for(j = 0;j < c2;j++)
            scanf("%d",&y[i][j]);
    for(i = 0;i < r1;i++)
    {
        for(j = 0;j < c2;j++)
        {
            z[i][j] = 0;
```

```
                for(k = 0;k < c1;k++)
                {
                    z[i][j] += x[i][k] * y[k][j];
                }
            }
        }
        printf("\n\nGiven matrix 1 is\n");
        for(i = 0;i < r1;i++)
        {
            printf("\n");
            for(j = 0;j < c1;j++)
                printf("%d\t",x[i][j]);
        }
        printf("\n\nGiven matrix 2 is\n");
        for(i = 0;i < r2;i++)
        {
            printf("\n");
            for(j = 0;j < c2;j++)
                printf("%d\t",y[i][j]);
        }

        printf("\n\nResultant matrix is\n");
        for(i = 0;i < r1;i++)
        {
            printf("\n");
            for(j = 0;j < c2;j++)
                printf("%d\t",z[i][j]);
        }
    }
```

22. Program to transpose the matrix

```
#include <stdio.h>

void main()
{
    int x[10][10], y[10][10], i, j, r, c;
    printf("\nEnter number of rows and columns\n");
    scanf("%d%d",&r,&c);
    printf("\nEnter %dx%d matrix values\n",r,c);
    for(i = 0;i < r;i++)
    {
        for(j = 0;j < c;j++)
        {
            scanf("%d",&x[i][j]);
            y[j][i] = x[i][j];
        }
    }
    printf("\nGiven matrix is\n");
    for(i = 0;i < r;i++) {
        printf("\n");
        for(j = 0;j < c;j++)
            printf("%d\t",x[i][j]);
    }
```

```
        printf("\nTranspose matrix is\n");
        for(i = 0;i < c;i++)
        {
            printf("\n");
            for(j = 0;j < r;j++)
                printf("%d\t",y[i][j]);
        }
}
```

23. Program to find the sum of diagonal & off diagonal elements in the matrix

```
#include <stdio.h>

void main()
{
    int x[10][10], i, j, ord, dsum = 0, odsum = 0;
    printf("\nEnter order of the matrix: ");
    scanf("%d",&ord);
    printf("\nEnter %dx%d matrix values\n",ord,ord);
    for(i = 0;i < ord;i++)
        for(j = 0;j < ord;j++)
            scanf("%d",&x[i][j]);
    for(i = 0, j = ord - 1;i < ord;i++, j--)
    {
        dsum += x[i][i];
        odsum += x[i][j];
    }
    printf("\nGiven matrix is\n");
    for(i = 0;i < ord;i++)
    {
        printf("\n");
        for(j = 0;j < ord;j++)
            printf("%d\t",x[i][j]);
    }
    printf("\nDiagonal sum is %d",dsum);
    printf("\nOff diagonal sum is %d",odsum);
}
```

24. Program to understand the two dimensional character array

```
#include <stdio.h>

void main()
{
    char name[5][30] = { "Dennis M. Ritchie", "Brian W. Kernighan", "Bjarne Stroustrup",
                    "James Gosling", "Anders Hejlsberg"};
    int i;
    for(i = 0;i < 5;i++)
        printf("\n%s",name[i]);
}
```

25. Program to read & print the 'n' different strings (Note: may be a collection of names, addresses, and etc.)

```
#include <stdio.h>

void main()
{
    char name[50][30];
    int i, n;
    printf("\nEnter number of string(s): ");
    scanf("%d",&n);
    printf("\nEnter %d string(s)\n",n);
    for(i = 0;i < n;i++)
        scanf("%s",name[i]);
    printf("\nGiven string(s) are\n");
    for(i = 0;i < n;i++)
        printf("\n%s",name[i]);
}
```

26. Program to sort the given list of numbers using bubble sort technique

```
#include <stdio.h>

void main()
{
    int x[50], n, i, j, t;
    printf("\nEnter how many number(s): ");
    scanf("%d",&n);
    printf("\nEnter %d number(s)\n",n);
    for(i=0;i < n;i++)
        scanf("%d",&x[i]);
    for(i = 1;i < n;i++)
    {
        for(j = 0;j < n - i;j++)
        {
            if(x[j] > x[j+1])
            {
                t = x[j];
                x[j] = x[j+1];
                x[j+1] = t;
            }
        }
    }
    printf("\nSorted number(s) are");
    for(i = 0;i < n;i++)
        printf("\n%d",x[i]);
}
```

27. Program to sort the given list of numbers using selection sort technique

```
#include <stdio.h>
```

```c
void main()
{
    int x[50], n, i, j, t;
    printf("\nEnter how many number(s): ");
    scanf("%d",&n);
    printf("\nEnter %d number(s)\n",n);
    for(i=0;i < n;i++)
        scanf("%d",&x[i]);
    for(i = 0;i < n - 1;i++)
    {
        for(j = i + 1;j < n;j++)
        {
            if(x[i] > x[j])
            {
                t = x[i];
                x[i] = x[j];
                x[j] = t;
            }
        }
    }
    printf("\nSorted number(s) are");
    for(i = 0;i < n;i++)
        printf("\n%d",x[i]);
}
```

28. Program to sort the given list of names using bubble sort technique

```c
#include <stdio.h>
#include <string.h>

void main() {
    int n, i, j;
    char name[50][30], t[30];
    printf("\nEnter how many name(s): ");
    scanf("%d",&n);
    printf("\nEnter %d name(s)\n",n);
    for(i=0;i < n;i++)
        scanf("%s",name[i]);
    for(i = 0;i < n - 1;i++)
    {
        for(j = i + 1;j < n;j++)
        {
            if(strcmp(name[i],name[j]) > 0)
            {
                strcpy(t,name[i]);
                strcpy(name[i],name[j]);
                strcpy(name[j],t);
            }
        }
    }
    printf("\nSorted name(s) are");
    for(i = 0;i < n;i++)
        printf("\n%s",name[i]);
}
```

29. Program to find the median and range of a set of numbers

```c
#include <stdio.h>

void main()
{
    float x[50], median, range;
    int n, i, j, t;
    printf("\nEnter how many number(s): ");
    scanf("%d",&n);
    printf("\nEnter %d number(s)\n",n);
    for(i = 0;i < n;i++)
        scanf("%f",&x[i]);
    for(i = 1;i < n;i++)
    {
        for(j = 0;j < n - i;j++)
        {
            if(x[j] > x[j+1])
            {
                t = x[j];
                x[j] = x[j+1];
                x[j+1] = t;
            }
        }
    }
    if(n%2 == 1)
        median = x[n / 2];
    else
        median = (x[n / 2 - 1] + x[n / 2]) / 2;

    range = x[n - 1] - x[0];
    printf("\nSorted number(s) are");
    for(i = 0;i < n;i++)
    {
        printf("\n%f",x[i]);
    }
    printf("\nMedian = %f",median);
    printf("\nRange = %f",range);
}
```

30. Program to sort the characters in the given string

```c
#include <stdio.h>
#include <string.h>

void main()
{
    char str[100], t;
    int n, i, j;
    printf("\nEnter string\n");
    gets(str);
```

```
n = strlen(str);
for(i = 1;i < n;i++)
{
      for(j = 0;j < n - i;j++)
      {
            if(str[j] > str [j+1])
            {
                  t = str[j];
                  str[j] = str[j+1];
                  str[j+1] = t;
            }
      }
}
printf("\nSorted characters are");
printf("\n%s",str);
}
```

31. Program to search the name from the list of names

```
#include <stdio.h>
#include <string.h>

void main()
{
      char name[50][30], fstr[30];
      int i, n;
      printf("\nEnter number of name(s): ");
      scanf("%d",&n);
      printf("\nEnter %d name(s)\n",n);
      for(i = 0;i < n;i++)
      {
            scanf("%s",name[i]);
      }
      printf("\nEnter the name to search: ");
      scanf("%s",fstr);
      for(i = 0;i < n;i++)
      {
            if(stricmp(name[i],fstr) == 0)
            {

                  printf("\n%s is found at %d",fstr,i+1);
                  break;
            }
      }
      if(i == n)
      {
            printf("\n%s is not found",fstr);
      }
}
```

32. Program to read & print the roll number & name of the two students

```c
#include <stdio.h>

void main()
{
    int rollno1, rollno2;
    char name1[30], name2[30];
    printf("\nEnter student 1 roll number and name\n");
    scanf("%d%s",&rollno1,name1);
    printf("\nEnter student 2 roll number and name\n");
    scanf("%d%s",&rollno2,name2);
    printf("\nStudent 1\nRoll number = %d",rollno1);
    printf("\nName = %s",name1);
    printf("\nStudent 2\nRoll number = %d",rollno2);
    printf("\nName = %s",name2);
}
```

5 STRUCTURE AND UNION PROGRAMS

1. Program to initialize & print the structure elements

```
#include <stdio.h>

struct stud
{
    int rollno;
    char name[40];
};

void main()
{
    struct stud s = {123, "Ram"};
    printf("\nRoll number = %d",s.rollno);
    printf("\nName = %s",s.name);
}
```

2. Program to read & print the roll number & name of the two students

```
#include <stdio.h>

struct stud
{
    int rollno;
    char name[40];
};

void main()
{
    struct stud s1, s2;
    printf("\nEnter student 1 roll number: ");
    scanf("%d",&s1.rollno);
    printf("\nEnter student 1 name\n");
    scanf("%s",s1.name);
    printf("\nEnter student 2 roll number and name\n");
    scanf("%d%s",&s2.rollno,s2.name);
```

```
        printf("\nStudent 1\nRoll number = %d",s1.rollno);
        printf("\nName = %s",s1.name);
        printf("\nStudent 2\nRoll number = %d",s2.rollno);
        printf("\nName = %s",s2.name);
}
```

3. Program to initialize & print the array of structure

```
#include <stdio.h>

struct stud
{
    int rollno;
    char name[40];
};

void main()
{
    struct stud s[3] = { {123, "Ram"}, {213, "Abdul"}, {321, "Charles"} };
    int i;
    for(i = 0;i < 3;i++)
        printf("\nStudent %d\nRoll number = %d\nName =  %s\n",i+1,s[i].rollno,s[i].name);
}
```

4. Program to read & print the 'n' students roll number & name

```
#include <stdio.h>

struct stud
{
    int rollno;
    char name[40];
};

void main()
{
    struct stud s[15];
    int n, i;
    printf("Enter number of student(s): ");
    scanf("%d",&n);
    printf("\nEnter %d student(s) details\n",n);
    for(i = 0;i < n;i++)
    {
        printf("\nGive student %d roll number and name\n",i+1);
        scanf("%d%s",&s[i].rollno,s[i].name);
    }
    for(i = 0;i < n;i++)
        printf("\nStudent %d\nRoll number = %d\nName = %s\n",i+1,s[i].rollno,s[i].name);
}
```

S.ANBAZHAGAN

5. Program to understand the structure within structure / nested structure

/* Method 1 */

```c
#include <stdio.h>

struct date
{
    int dd;
    int mm;
    int yyyy;
};

struct emp
{
    int no;
    char name[30];
    struct date doj;
};

void main()
{
    struct emp e;
    printf("\nEnter employee number, name and date of joining\n");
    scanf("%d%s%d%d%d",&e.no,e.name,&e.doj.dd, &e.doj.mm,&e.doj.yyyy);
    printf("\nEmployee number = %d",e.no);
    printf("\nName = %s",e.name);
    printf("\nDate of joining = %d-%d-%d",e.doj.dd,e.doj.mm,e.doj.yyyy);
}
```

/* Method 2 */

```c
#include <stdio.h>

struct emp
{
    int no;
    char name[30];
    struct date
    {
        int dd;
        int mm;
        int yyyy;
    } doj;
};

void main()
{
    struct emp e;
    printf("\nEnter employee number, name and date of joining\n");
    scanf("%d%s%d%d%d",&e.no,e.name,&e.doj.dd,&e.doj.mm,&e.doj.yyyy);
    printf("\nEmployee number = %d",e.no);
    printf("\nName = %s",e.name);
    printf("\nDate of joining = %d-%d-%d",e.doj.dd,e.doj.mm,e.doj.yyyy);
}
```

6. Program to understand the union

```c
#include <stdio.h>

struct st_data {
    char c;
    int i;
    float f;
    double d;
};

union uni_data {
    char c;
    int i;
    float f;
    double d;
};

void main()
{
    struct st_data s;
    union uni_data u;
    printf("\nMemory size occupied by uni_data: %d",sizeof(u));
    printf("\nMemory size occupied by st_data: %d", sizeof(s));
}
```

7. Program to create the register using union & structure

```c
#include <stdio.h>

union reg
{
    int r;
    struct
    {
        char l;
        char h;
    } x;
};

void main()
{
    union reg a;
    a.r = 257;
    printf("\nRegister A = %d",a.r);
    printf("\nRegister AL = %d",a.x.l);
    printf("\nRegister AH = %d",a.x.h);
    a.x.l = 5;
    a.x.h = 1;
    printf("\nRegister A = %d",a.r);
    printf("\nRegister AL = %d",a.x.l);
    printf("\nRegister AH = %d",a.x.h);
}
```

6 POINTER PROGRAMS

1. Program to understand the memory size of the pointers

```
#include <stdio.h>

struct stud
{
    int rollno;
    char name[40];
};

void main()
{
    int *ip;
    char *cp;
    float *fp;
    double *dp;
    struct stud *sp;
    printf("\nIP size = %d",sizeof(ip));
    printf("\nCP size = %d",sizeof(cp));
    printf("\nFP size = %d",sizeof(fp));
    printf("\nDP size = %d",sizeof(dp));
    printf("\nSP size = %d",sizeof(sp));
}
```

2. Program to understand the displacement of the pointers

```
#include <stdio.h>

struct stud
{
    int rollno;
    char name[40];
};

void main()
{
    int *ip = 0;
    char *cp = 0;
```

```
        float *fp = 0;
        double *dp = 0;
        struct stud *sp = 0;
        printf("\nIP = %u",ip);
        printf("\nCP = %u",cp);
        printf("\nFP = %u",fp);
        printf("\nDP = %u",dp);
        ip++;
        cp++;
        fp++;
        dp++;
        sp++;
        printf("\nNow, IP = %u",ip);
        printf("\nNow, CP = %u",cp);
        printf("\nNow, FP = %u",fp);
        printf("\nNow, DP = %u",dp);
        printf("\nNow, SP = %u",sp);
}
```

3. Program to understand the pointer to variable

/* Program 1 */

```
#include <stdio.h>

void main() {
        int x, *ip;
        x = 10;
        printf("\nX value = %d",x);
        printf("\nX address = %u",&x);
        ip = &x;
        printf("\nX value = %d",*ip);
        printf("\nX address = %u",ip);
        *ip = 15;
        printf("\nNow, X value = %d",x);
}
```

/* Program 2 */

```
#include <stdio.h>

void main() {
        int x, *ip;
        x = 33;
        ip = &x;
        *ip = 20;
        printf("\nX value = %d",x);
        printf("\nX value = %d",*ip);
        printf("\nX value = %d",*&x);
        printf("\nX value = %d",**&ip);
        printf("\nX address = %u",&x);
        printf("\nX address = %u",ip);
        printf("\nX address = %u",*&ip);
}
```

4. Program to understand the pointer to one dimensional array

```c
#include <stdio.h>

void main()
{
    int e[3] = {1, 12, 123}, i, *ip;
    ip = e;
    for(i=0;i<3;i++)
    {
        printf("\ne[%d] address = %u %u %u %u %u %u",i,&e[i],&i[e],ip+i,i+ip,e+i,i+e);
        printf("\ne[%d] value = %d %d %d %d %d %d",i,e[i],i[e],*(ip+i),*(i+ip),*(e+i),*(i+e));
    }
}
```

5. Program to understand the pointer to string

```c
#include <stdio.h>

void main()
{
    char str[] = "Welcome", *cp;
    cp = str;
    while(*cp != '\0')
    {
        printf("\n%u str[%d] = %c",cp,cp-str,*cp);
        cp++;
    }
}
```

6. Program to understand the pointer to two dimensional array

```c
#include <stdio.h>

void main()
{
    int array[3][3]={{1, 2, 3},{1, 1, 1},{3, 2, 1}}, i, j, *p;
    p = array;
    for(i = 0;i < 3;i++)
    {
        for(j = 0;j < 3;j++,p++)
        {
            printf("\narray[%d][%d] addr. = %u %u %u",i,j,&array[i][j],*(array+i)+j,p);
            printf("\narray[%d][%d] value = %d %d %d",i,j,array[i][j], *(*(array+i)+j),*p);
        }
    }
}
```

7. Program to understand the pointer to structure

```c
#include <stdio.h>

struct stud
{
    int rollno;
    char name[15];
    int age;
};

void main()
{
    struct stud s = {100, "Ram", 20}, *sp;
    printf("\nRoll number = %d",s.rollno);
    printf("\nName        = %s",s.name);
    printf("\nAge         = %d",s.age);
    sp = &s;
    sp->age = 21;
    strcpy(sp->name,"Rama");
    printf("\nSize(s): %d\nSize(sp): %d",sizeof(s),sizeof(sp));
    printf("\nRoll number = %d",s.rollno);
    printf("\nName        = %s",sp->name);
    printf("\nAge         = %d",(*sp).age);
}
```

7 FUNCTION PROGRAMS

1. Program to understand the concepts of no return value and no argument function

/* Method 1 */

```
#include <stdio.h>

void printmyname();  /* Function Declaration */

void main()
{
    printmyname();   /* Calling Function */
    printmyname();
    printmyname();
}

                       /* Called Function */
void printmyname()   /* Function Definition */
{
    printf("\nDennis M. Ritchie");
}
```

/* Method 2 */

```
#include <stdio.h>

                       /* Called Function */
void printmyname()   /* Function Definition */
{
    printf("\nDennis M. Ritchie");
}

void main()
{
    printmyname();  /* Calling Function */
    printmyname();
    printmyname();
}
```

2. Program to understand the concepts of no return value and no argument function

```c
#include <stdio.h>

void printline()
{
    int i;
    printf("\n");
    for(i=1;i<=80;i++)
        printf("-");
}

void main()
{
    printline();
    printf("\t\t\tC Programming Language Author(s)");
    printline();
    printf("\t\t1. nBrian W. Kernighan\n");
    printf("\t\t2. Dennis M. Ritchie\n");
    printline();
}
```

3. Program to understand the concepts of no return value with argument function

```c
/* Program 1 */

#include <stdio.h>

void printline(char c)
{
    int i;
    printf("\n");
    for(i=1;i<=80;i++)
        printf("%c",c);
}

void main()
{
    char ch='$';
    printline('a');
    printf("\t\t\tC Programming Language Author(s)");
    printline(ch);
    printf("\t\t1. nBrian W. Kernighan\n");
    printf("\t\t2. Dennis M. Ritchie\n");
    printline();
    printline('*');
}
```

```c
/* Program 2 */

#include <stdio.h>
```

```
void printline(char c, int n)
{
    int i;
    printf("\n");
    for(i=1;i<=n;i++)
        printf("%c",c);
}

void main()
{
    char ch='$';
    int n = 55;
    printline('a', 60);
    printf("\t\t\tC Programming Language Author(s)");
    printline(ch, n);
    printf("\t\t1. nBrian W. Kernighan\n");
    printf("\t\t2. Dennis M. Ritchie\n");
    printline();
    printline('*', 50);
}
```

4. Program to understand the concepts of return value without argument function

```
#include <stdio.h>

void ret143()
{
    return 143;
}

void main()
{
    int n = 0;
    printf("\nBefore, calling function N = %d\n",n);
    n = ret143();
    printf("\nAfter, calling function N = %d\n",n);
}
```

5. Program to understand the concepts of return value without argument function

```
#include <stdio.h>

double cube(double n)
{
    double r;
    r = n * n * n;   /* return n*n*n; */
    return r;
}

void main()
{
    double n, res;
```

```
        printf("\nEnter number to find cube: ");
        scanf("%lf", &n);
        res = cube(n);
        printf("\nCUBE( %lf ) = %lf\n", n, res);
}
```

6. Program to find the factorial using function

```
#include <stdio.h>

long int fact(int n)
{
    int i;
    long int f=1;
    for(i=1;i<=n;i++)
        f=f*i;
    return f;
}

void main()
{
    int n;
    long f;
    printf("\nEnter N Value: ");
    scanf("%d",&n);
    f = fact(n);
    printf("\nFactorial of %d is %ld",n,f);
    f = fact(5);
    printf("\nFactorial of 5 is %ld",f);
}
```

7. Program to calculate the average of three numbers using function

```
#include <stdio.h>

float avg3(int x,int y,int z)
{
 float r;
 r = (x+y+z)/3.0;   /* return (x+y+z)/3.0; */
 return r;
}

void main()
{
    int a,b,c;
    float d;
    printf("\nEnter three numbers\n");
    scanf("%d%d%d",&a,&b,&c);
    d = avg3(a,b,c);
    printf("\nAverage = %f",d);
}
```

8. Program to perform nCr combinations calculation. nCr = n! / (r! * (n-r)!)

```c
#include <stdio.h>

long int fact(int n)
{
    int i;
    long int f=1;
    for(i=1;i<=n;i++)
        f=f*i;
    return f;
}

void main()
{
    int n,r;
    long res;
    printf("\nEnter N Value : ");
    scanf("%d",&n);
    printf("\nEnter R Value : ");
    scanf("%d",&r);
    res = fact(n) /( fact(r) * fact(n-r) );
    printf("\nC(%d, %d) = %ld", n, r, res);
}
```

9. Program to find the 'x' to the power 'n' using function

```c
#include <stdio.h>

float power(float x,int n)
{
    float ans=1.0;
    int i;
    for(i=1;i<=n;i++)
        ans = ans * x;
    return ans;
}

void main()
{
    int n;
    float x,res;
    printf("\nEnter X Value: ");
    scanf("%f",&x);
    printf("\nEnter N Value: ");
    scanf("%d",&n);
    res = power(x,n);
    printf("\n%.2f to the power %d is = %.2f",x,n,res);
    res = power(x,2);
    printf("\n%.2f to the power 2 is = %.2f",x,res);
    res = power(2,n);
    printf("\n2 to the power %d is = %.2f",n,res);
}
```

10. Prerequisite program to understand the concepts of call by value

```c
#include <stdio.h>

void main()
{
    int a = 10;
    int x = a;
    printf("\nA = %d",a);
    printf("\nX = %d",x);
    x++;
    printf("\nA = %d",a);
    printf("\nX = %d",x);
}
```

11. Program to understand the concepts of call by value

```c
#include <stdio.h>

void change(int x)   /*   x is dummy argument or formal argument */
{
    x = x + 10;
}

void main()
{
    int a;
    printf("\nGive A = ");
    scanf("%d",&a);
    printf("\nBefore Calling Function, A = %d",a);
    change(a);      /*    a is original argument or actual argument */
    printf("\nAfter Calling Function, A = %d",a);
}
```

12. Prerequisite program to understand the concepts of call by reference

```c
#include <stdio.h>

void main()
{
    int a = 10;
    int *x = &a;

    printf("\nA = %d",a);
    printf("\nX = %d",*x);
    (*x)++;
    printf("\nA = %d",a);
    printf("\nX = %d",*x);
}
```

13. Program to understand the concepts of call by reference

```c
#include <stdio.h>

void change(int *x)  /*   x is dummy argument or formal argument */
{
    *x = *x + 10;
}

void main()
{
    int n;
    printf("\nGive N = ");
    scanf("%d",&n);
    printf("\nBefore Calling Function, N = %d",n);
    change(&n);    /*   n is original argument or actual argument */
    printf("\nAfter Calling Function, N = %d",n);
}
```

14. Program to calculate the sum and average of three numbers using function and call by reference

```c
#include <stdio.h>

void sumavg3(int x,int y,int z,int *s,float *a)
{
    *s = x + y + z;
    *a = *s / 3.0;
}

void main()
{
    int a,b,c,sum=0;
    float avg=0;
    printf("\nGive A, B and C values\n");
    scanf("%d%d%d",&a,&b,&c);
    printf("\nSum = %d",sum);
    printf("\nAverage = %f",avg);
    sumavg3(a,b,c,&sum,&avg);
    printf("\nSum = %d",sum);
    printf("\nAverage = %f",avg);
}
```

15. Program to understand the concepts of passing array as argument

```c
#include <stdio.h>

void change(int x[],int n)
{
    int i;
    for(i=0;i<n;i++)
        x[i] = x[i] + 10;
}
```

```
void main()
{
    int arr[5]={1,2,3,4,5},i;
    printf("\nBefore Calling Fun., Array Values are\n");
    for(i=0;i<5;i++)
        printf("\n%d",arr[i]);
    change(arr,5);
    printf("\nAfter Calling Fun., Array Values are\n");
    for(i=0;i<5;i++)
        printf("\n%d",arr[i]);
}
```

16. Program to understand the concepts of passing structure as argument

/* Program 1 */

```
#include <stdio.h>

struct person
{
    char name[30];
    int age;
};

void printperson(struct person p)
{
    printf("\nName = %s",p.name);
    printf("\nAge = %d",p.age);
}

void main()
{
    struct person p1,p2;
    printf("Enter Person 1 Name and Age\n");
    scanf("%s%d",p1.name,&p1.age);
    printf("Enter Person 2 Name and Age\n");
    scanf("%s%d",p2.name,&p2.age);
    printperson(p1);
    printperson(p2);
}
```

/* Program 2 */

```
#include <stdio.h>

struct person
{
    char name[30];
    int age;
};
```

```
void printperson(struct person p)
{
     printf("\nName = %s",p.name);
     printf("\nAge = %d",p.age);
}

void readperson(struct person *p)
{
     printf("\nEnter Person Name and Age\n");
     scanf("%s%d",p->name,&p->age);
}

void main()
{
     struct person p1,p2;
     readperson(&p1);
     readperson(&p2);
     printperson(p1);
     printperson(p2);
}
```

8 RECURSION AND SCOPE RULE PROGRAMS

1. Program to find the factorial using recursive function

```c
#include <stdio.h>

long int fact(int n)
{
    if(n==0 || n==1)
        return 1;
    return n * fact(n-1);
}

void main()
{
    int n;
    long res;
    printf("Enter N Value : ");
    scanf("%d",&n);
    res = fact(n);
    printf("\nFactorial of %d is %ld",n,res);
}
```

2. Program to find the gcd using recursive function

```c
#include <stdio.h>

int gcd(int x,int y)
{
    if(y == 0)
        return x;
    else if(y > x)
        gcd(y,x);
    else
        gcd(y,x%y);
}
```

```c
void main()
{
    int a,b,r;
    printf("\nEnter two numbers\n");
    scanf("%d%d",&a,&b);
    r = gcd(a,b);
    printf("\nGCD(%d,%d) = %d",a,b,r);
    printf("\nGCD(10,15) = %d",gcd(10,15));
}
```

3. Program to print the integer number using recursive function

```c
#include <stdio.h>
void printd(int n)
{
    if(n < 0)
    {
        n = -n;
        putchar('-');
    }
    if(n/10)
        printd(n/10);
    putchar('0'+n%10);
}

void main()
{
    int x;
    printf("Enter x value : ");
    scanf("%d",&x);
    printd(x);
}
```

4. Program to understand the concepts of local or automatic variable

```c
#include <stdio.h>

void fun()
{
    auto int i=15;
    printf("\nI = %d",i);
}

void main()
{
    auto int i;
    printf("\nI = %d",i);
    i=10;
    printf("\nI = %d",i);
```

```
    fun();
    printf("\nI = %d",i);
    {
        auto int i=5;
        printf("\nI = %d",i);
        {
            auto int i=25;
            printf("\nI = %d",i);
        }
        printf("\nI = %d",i);
    }
    printf("\nI = %d",i);
    fun();
}
```

5. Program to understand the concepts of external or global variable

```
#include <stdio.h>

void fun()
{
    i=i+15;
}

int i;

void main()
{
    printf("\nI = %d",i);
    fun();
    printf("\nI = %d",i);
    {
        auto int i=2;
        printf("\nI = %d",i);
    }
    printf("\nI = %d",i);
    fun();
    printf("\nI = %d",i);
}
```

6. Program to understand the concepts of static variable

```
#include <stdio.h>

void fun()
{
    static int i;
    i++; /*i=i+1*/
    printf("\nI = %d",i);
}
```

```
void main()
{
    fun();
    fun();
    fun();
    fun();
}
```

7. Program to understand the concepts of register variable

```
#include <stdio.h>

void main()
{
    register int i;
    printf("\nI = %d",i);
    for(i=1;i<=100;i++)
        printf("\n%d",i);
}
```

9 FILES AND COMMAND LINE ARGUMENTS PROGRAMS

1. Prerequisite program to understand the concepts of file handling

```
#include <stdio.h>

void main()
{
    int i,j;
    for(i=0;i<=255;i++)
    {
        printf("%d -----> %c\n",i,i);
    }
}
```

2. Program to understand the concepts of file writing

```
#include <stdio.h>

void main()
{
    FILE *fp;
    fp=fopen("cexpert.dat","w");
    fprintf(fp,"Dennis M. Ritchie\n");
    fprintf(fp,"Brian W. Kernighan\n");
    fprintf(fp,"Ken Thompson\n");
    fprintf(fp,"Bjarne Stroustrup\n");
    fclose(fp);
}
```

3. Program to print the ASCII table to file

```
#include <stdio.h>

void main()
{
    FILE *fp;
    int i;
    fp=fopen("ascii.dat","w");
```

```
    for(i=0;i<256;i++)
        fprintf(fp,"%d -----> %c\n",i,i);
    fclose(fp);
}
```

4. Program to read the specified file contents

```
#include <stdio.h>

void main()
{
    char fn[30];
    FILE *fp;
    char ch;
    printf("Enter file name: ");
    scanf("%s",fn);
    fp = fopen(fn,"r");
    if(fp == NULL)
    {
        printf("\nFile not found");
        return;
    }
    do
    {
        ch = fgetc(fp);
        printf("%c",ch);
    } while(!feof(fp));
    fclose(fp);
}
```

5. Program to calculate the sum and average of numbers from val.dat file. The contents of val.dat is
```
    10
    45
    78
    ...
```

```
#include <stdio.h>

void main()
{
    FILE *fp;
    int x,sum=0,n=0;
    float avg;
    fp=fopen("val.dat","r");
    if(fp==NULL)
    {
        printf("\nFile not found");
        return;
    }
```

```
    do
    {
        fscanf(fp,"%d",&x);
        printf("%d\n",x);
        sum+=x;
        n++;
    } while(!feof(fp));
    avg = sum / (float)n;
    printf("\nN = %d",n);
    printf("\nSum = %d",sum);
    printf("\nAverage = %f",avg);
}
```

6. Program to understand the concepts of binary file writing and reading

```
#include <stdio.h>

void main()
{
    FILE *fp;
    char a;
    int b;
    float c;
    double d;
    fp = fopen("test.bin", "wb");
    a = 'A';
    b = 123;
    c = 1.23;
    d = 12.3;
    fwrite(&a, sizeof(a), 1, fp);
    fwrite(&b, sizeof(b), 1, fp);
    fwrite(&c, sizeof(c), 1, fp);
    fwrite(&d, sizeof(d), 1, fp);
    fclose(fp);
    if((fp = fopen("test.bin", "rb")) == NULL)
    {
        printf("\nFile not found");
        return;
    }
    fread(&a, sizeof(a), 1, fp);
    fread(&b, sizeof(b), 1, fp);
    fread(&c, sizeof(c), 1, fp);
    fread(&d, sizeof(d), 1, fp);
    printf("\nA = %c",a);
    printf("\nB = %d",b);
    printf("\nC = %f",c);
    printf("\nD = %lf",d);
    fclose(fp);
}
```

7. Program to understand the concepts of random access file handling

```c
#include <stdio.h>

void main()
{
    FILE *fp;
    char c;
    int i=0;
    fp = fopen("alpha.dat","w");
    while(!feof(fp))
    {
        fseek(fp,i,SEEK_CUR);
        c = fgetc(fp);
        putchar(c);
        i = i + 5;
    }
    fseek(fp,-2,SEEK_END);
    c = fgetc(fp);
    putchar(c);
    fseek(fp,0,SEEK_SET);
    printf("\n%d",ftell(fp));
    fseek(fp,0,SEEK_END);
    printf("\nFile Size %d",ftell(fp));
    fclose(fp);
}
```

8. Program to understand the concepts of command line arguments

```c
#include <stdio.h>
void main(int argc,char *argv[])
{
    int i;
    printf("Number of Argument is %d",argc);
    for(i=0;i<argc;i++)
        printf("\n%s",argv[i]);
}
```

9. Program to read the specified file contents using command line arguments

```c
#include <stdio.h>
void main(int argc,char *argv[])
{
    FILE *fp;
    char ch;
    if(argc!=2)
    {
        printf("Usage: FREAD <file_name>");
        return;
    }
```

```
fp = fopen(argv[1],"r");
if(fp==NULL)
{
     printf("The file %s is not found",argv[1]);
     return;
}
do
{
     ch = fgetc(fp);
     putchar(ch);
} while(!feof(fp));
fclose(fp);
}
```

10 MISCELLANEOUS PROGRAMS

1. Program to read the 'n' numbers & print the same using dynamic memory management

```c
#include <stdio.h>
#include <alloc.h>

void main()
{
    int n, i, *x;
    printf("\nEnter how many number(s): ");
    scanf("%d",&n);
    x = malloc(n * sizeof(int));
    if(x == NULL)
    {
        printf("\nError in memory allocation");
        return;
    }
    printf("\nEnter %d number(s)\n",n);
    for(i = 0;i < n;i++)
        scanf("%d",x+i);
    for(i = 0;i < n;i++)
        printf("\nElement %d = %d",i+1,x[i]);
    free(x);
}
```

2. Program to understand the concepts of type casting

```c
#include <stdio.h>
void main()
{
    int totMarks = 350, noOfSub = 5;
    float per;
    per = totMarks / noOfSub;
    printf("\nPercentage: %f",per);
    per = (float) totMarks / noOfSub;
    printf("\nPercentage: %f",per);
}
```

3. Program to understand the concepts of const keyword

```c
#include <stdio.h>

void main()
{
    const float PI = 3.14;
    float rad = 1.0, area;
    area = PI * rad * rad;
    printf("\nArea of circle is %f",area);
}
```

4. Program to understand the concepts of typedef keyword

```c
#include <stdio.h>

typedef struct student
{
    int rollno;
    char name[40];
} stud;

void main()
{
    stud s = {123, "Ram"};
    printf("\nRoll number = %d",s.rollno);
    printf("\nName = %s",s.name);
}
```

5. Program to understand the concepts of pragma preprocessor

```c
#include <stdio.h>

void initFun()
{
    printf("\nAllocate the dyanamic memory here");
}

void relFun()
{
    printf("\nDeallocate the memory here");
}

#pragma startup initFun
#pragma exit relFun

void main()
{
    printf("\n#PRAGMA Start");
    printf("\n#PRAGMA End");
}
```

6. Program to understand the concepts predefined macros

```
#include <stdio.h>

void main()
{
    printf("\nFILE: %s",__FILE__);
    printf("\nDATE: %s",__DATE__);
    printf("\nTIME: %s",__TIME__);
}
```

7. Program to understand the concepts of bit field declaration in structure definition

```
#include <stdio.h>

struct
{
    unsigned char bin : 1;
    unsigned char oct : 3;
    unsigned char hex : 4;
} base;

void main()
{
    printf("\nBytes occupied: %d",sizeof(base));
    base.bin = 1;
    printf("\nbase.bin = %d",base.bin);
    base.bin = 2;
    printf("\nbase.bin = %d",base.bin);
    base.oct = 5;
    printf("\nbase.oct = %d",base.oct);
    base.oct = 7;
    printf("\nbase.oct = %d",base.oct);
    base.oct = 9;
    printf("\nbase.oct = %d",base.oct);
    base.hex = 9;
    printf("\nbase.hex = %d",base.hex);
    base.hex = 15;
    printf("\nbase.hex = %d",base.hex);
    base.hex = 18;
    printf("\nbase.hex = %d",base.hex);
}
```

8. Program to understand the concepts of variable number of arguments

```
#include <stdio.h>
#include <stdarg.h>

double sum(int num, ...)
{
    va_list valist;
    double s = 0.0;
    int i;
```

```
        va_start(valist, num);
        for (i = 0; i < num; i++)
        {
                s = s + va_arg(valist, double);
        }
        va_end(valist);
        return s;
}

void main()
{
        double res;
        res = sum(3,10.0,15.0,20.0);
        printf("\nSum(10,15,20)=%lf",res);
        printf("\nSum(5,15)=%lf",sum(2,5.0,15.0));
}
```

9. Program to measure the total execution time of a program

```
#include<stdio.h>
#include<time.h>

void main()
{
        long int i;
        double total_time;
        clock_t start, end;
        start = clock();//time count starts
        for (i = 1; i <= 100000000; i++);
        end = clock();//time count stops
        total_time = ((double) (end - start)) / CLK_TCK;
        printf("\nTime taken: %f", total_time);
}
```

10. Program to swap the two numbers using macros

```
#include <stdio.h>
#define swap(x,y) x^=y^=x^=y

void main()
{
        int a, b;
        printf("\nEnter two numbers\n");
        scanf("%d%d",&a,&b);
        printf("\nBefore using macro,\nA is %d\nB is %d",a,b);
        swap(a,b);
        printf("\nAfter using macro,\nA is %d\nB is %d",a,b);
}
```

11. What will be the output of this program?

```
#include <stdio.h>

void main()
{
    int i;
    *&i = 10;
    printf("%d",i);
}
```

12. What will be the output of this program?

```
#include <stdio.h>

struct aaa
{
    struct aaa *prev;
    int i;
    struct aaa *next;
};

void main()
{
    struct aaa abc,def,ghi,jkl;
    int x = 100;
    abc.i = 0; abc.prev = &jkl; abc.next = &def;
    def.i = 1; def.prev = &abc; def.next = &ghi;
    ghi.i = 2; ghi.prev = &def; ghi.next = &jkl;
    jkl.i = 3; jkl.prev = &ghi; jkl.next = &abc;
    x = abc.next->next->prev->next->i;
    printf("%d",x);
}
```

13. What is the output of this program?

```
#include <stdio.h>

aaa()
{
    printf("Hi");
}

bbb()
{
    printf("Hello");
}

ccc()
{
    printf("Bye");
}
```

```
void main()
{
    int (*ptr[3])();
    ptr[0]=aaa;
    ptr[1]=bbb;
    ptr[2]=ccc;
    ptr[2]();
}
```

14. What will be the output of this program?

```
#include <stdio.h>

void main()
{
    union bbb
    {
        struct
        {
            int a:1;
            int b:1;
            int c:1;
            int d:1;
            int e:1;
            int f:1;
            int g:1;
            int h:1;
        } aaa;
        char x;
    };
    union bbb pqr;
    pqr.aaa.a=pqr.aaa.b=pqr.aaa.c=pqr.aaa.d=1;
    pqr.aaa.e=pqr.aaa.f=pqr.aaa.g=pqr.aaa.h=1 ;
    printf("%d",pqr.x);
}
```

15. What is the output of this program?

```
#include <stdio.h>

void main()
{
    int i=0;
    i=abc();
    printf("%d",i);
}

abc()
{
    _AX=1000;
}
```

16. What will be the output of this program?

```c
#include <stdio.h>

int i=5;

void main()
{
    int i=4;
    i=abc(i=i/4);
    printf("%d",i);
}

abc(int i)
{
    return (i/2);
}
```

17. What will be the output of this program?

```c
#include <stdio.h>

int i=5;

void main()
{
    int i=4;
    abc(i/4);
    printf("%d",i);
}

abc(int i)
{
    return (i/2);
}
```

18. What is the output of this program?

```c
#include <stdio.h>

struct xxx
{
    int i;
    char j;
};

void main()
{
    struct xxx zzz={10,65};
    abc(zzz);
}
```

```
abc(struct xxx a)
{
    printf("%d...%c",a.i,a.j);
}
```

19. C program to create your own header file

/* mymath.h – Header File */

```
#define max(x,y) (x)>(y) ? x : y
#define min(x,y) (x)<(y) ? x : y
#define sum(x,y) (x)+(y)
#define avg(x,y) (sum(x,y))/2
```

/* MAIN Source File */

```
#include <stdio.h>
#include "mymath.h"

void main()
{
    int a, b, res;
    printf("\nEnter two numbers\n");
    scanf("%d%d",&a,&b);
    res = max(a,b);
    printf("\nmax(%d,%d)=%d",a,b,res);
    res = min(a,b);
    printf("\nmin(%d,%d)=%d",a,b,res);
    res = sum(a,b);
    printf("\nsum(%d,%d)=%d",a,b,res);
    res = avg(a,b);
    printf("\navg(%d,%d)=%d",a,b,res);
}
```

APPENDIX – HOW TO INSTALL TURBO C++: COMPILE & RUN A C PROGRAM

The first thing you need to understand is that computer (Machine) can only understand Machine language (Stream of 0s and 1s). In order to convert your C program source code to Machine code, you need to compile it. The compiler is the one, which converts source code to Machine code. In simple terms, you can understand that a compiler converts the human readable code to a machine readable format.

A1.1 Install Turbo C++

Download Turbo C++ for Windows. After download, install the Turbo C++ in the location C:\tc.

A1.2 Compile & Run a C Program

Step 1: Locate the TC.exe file and open it. You will find it at location C:\TC\BIN\.

Step 2: File > New (as shown in below picture) and then write your C program

Step 3: Save the program using F2 (OR file > Save), remember the extension should be ".c". In the below screenshot I have given the name as first.c.

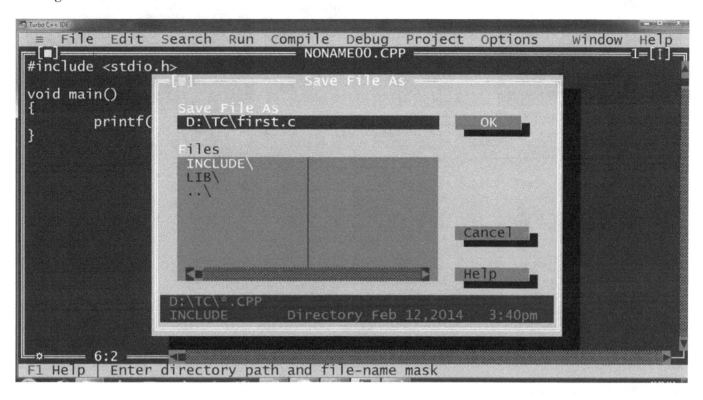

Step 4: Compile the program using Alt + F9 OR Compile > Compile (as shown in the below screenshot).

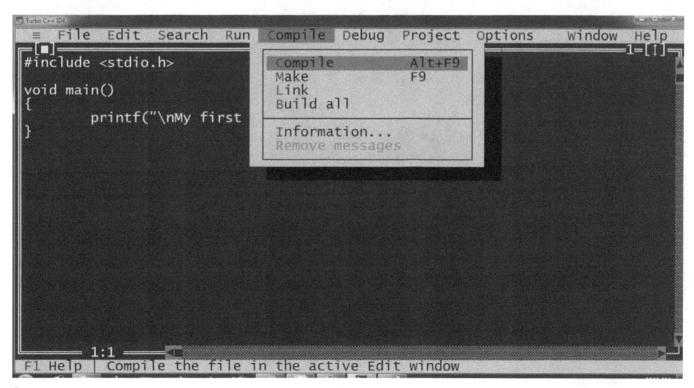

Step 5: Press Ctrl + F9 to Run (or select Run > Run in menu bar) the C program.

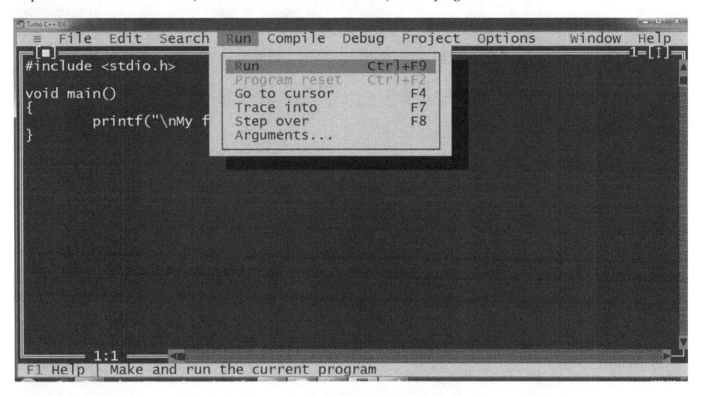

Step 6: Alt+F5 to view the output of the program on the output screen.

ABOUT THE AUTHOR

S.Anbazhagan was born in Mayiladuthurai, Tamil Nadu, India, on December 30, 1979. He received the Diploma in Computer Technology from Muthiah Polytechnic College, Annamalai Nagar, Chidambaram, Tamil Nadu, India, in 1997. He obtained his B.E. degree in Electrical Engineering in 2002, Post-Graduate Diploma in Computer Applications in 2004, M.E. degree in Computer Science and Engineering in 2009, and the Ph.D. degree in Computer Science and Engineering in 2015 from Annamalai University, Annamalai Nagar, Chidambaram, Tamil Nadu, India.

At present, he is an Assistant Professor in the Department of Electrical Engineering, Faculty of Engineering and Technology, Annamalai University, Annamalai Nagar, Chidambaram, India. He has published papers in 9 internationally reviewed journals and he has presented 6 international conference papers. His current research interests include computer programming languages, image processing, and soft computing techniques applied to various engineering problem domains.

Mr.S.Anbazhagan is an Associate of The Institution of Engineers (India) and a life member of the Indian Society of Technical Education. He received the best paper award at the IET-U.K. (formerly IEE) international conference in 2011. He appeared for GATE in 2009 and secured 87.77 percentile score. Also, he is a reviewer for the International Journal of Electrical Power & Energy Systems, Energy Conversion and Management, IET Generation, Transmission & Distribution, IEEE Transactions on Neural Networks and Learning Systems, IEEE Transactions on Power Systems, IEEE Transactions on Smart Grid and other international reputed journals.

www.ingramcontent.com/pod-product-compliance
Lightning Source LLC
Chambersburg PA
CBHW060202060326
40690CB00018B/4220